THE ROCK CYCLE AT WORK

By George Pendergast

Gareth Stevens
PUBLISHING

Please visit our website, www.garethstevens.com. For a free color catalog of all our high-quality books, call toll free 1-800-542-2595 or fax 1-877-542-2596.

Library of Congress Cataloging-in-Publication Data

Pendergast, George, author.
 The rock cycle at work / George Pendergast.
     pages cm. — (Cycles in nature)
 Includes bibliographical references and index.
 ISBN 978-1-4824-1667-1 (pbk.)
 ISBN 978-1-4824-1668-8 (6 pack)
 ISBN 978-1-4824-1666-4 (library binding)
 1. Geochemical cycles—Juvenile literature. 2. Geology, Structural—Juvenile literature.
 I. Title.
 QE501.25.P46 2015
 552—dc23

                                    2014034823

Published in 2016 by
Gareth Stevens Publishing
111 East 14th Street, Suite 349
New York, NY 10003

Copyright © 2016 Gareth Stevens Publishing

Designer: Sarah Liddell
Editor: Ryan Nagelhout

Photo credits: Cover, p. 1 Leene/Shutterstock.com; p. 5 Leksele/Shutterstock.com;
p. 7 (igneous) Lindsay Douglas/Shutterstock.com; p. 7 (sedimentary) mdd/Shutterstock.com;
pp. 7 (metamorphic), 17 Doug Lemke/Shutterstock.com; p. 9 Robert Crow/Shutterstock.com;
p. 11 (top) Chris Howey/Shutterstock.com; p. 11 (bottom) Sergejus Lamanosovas/
Shutterstock.com; p. 13 Tami Freed/Shutterstock.com; p. 15 dexns/Shutterstock.com;
p. 19 (limestone) Matthijs Wetterauw/Shutterstock.com; p. 19 (marble) Wiratchai
wansamngam/Shutterstock.com; p. 21 (background) altanaka/Shutterstock.com;
p. 21 (igneous) optimarc/Shutterstock.com; p. 21 (metamorphic) Fablok/Shutterstock.com;
p. 21 (sedimentary) michal812/Shutterstock.com.

Printed in the United States of America

CPSIA compliance information: Batch #CS16GS: For further information contact Gareth Stevens, New York, New York at 1-800-542-2595.

CONTENTS

Boldface words appear in the glossary.

The Rocky Road

The study of Earth's rocks and their history is called geology. Rocks are always changing. How rocks change is shaped by forces acting on them. Some rocks change very slowly, over millions of years. Others change very quickly.

5

Rocks go through changes to make different kinds of rocks. These events happen over and over. This is called the rock cycle. Heat, **pressure**, and water change rocks. The three different kinds of rocks are called **igneous** (IHG-nee-uhs), **sedimentary** (seh-duh-MEHN-tuh-ree), and **metamorphic** (meh-tuh-MOHR-fihk).

igneous rock

sedimentary rock

metamorphic rock

7

Lava Rocks

Most rocks start as igneous rocks. They're formed when hot, liquid rock inside Earth, called magma, cools. Sometimes igneous rock forms deep inside Earth. Sometimes it forms from magma that has reached Earth's surface as lava.

9

Igneous rocks can be smooth like glass. Some also have big **crystals** in them. Over time, different forces change rocks on the surface. Wind and rain can wear them down. This is called weathering.

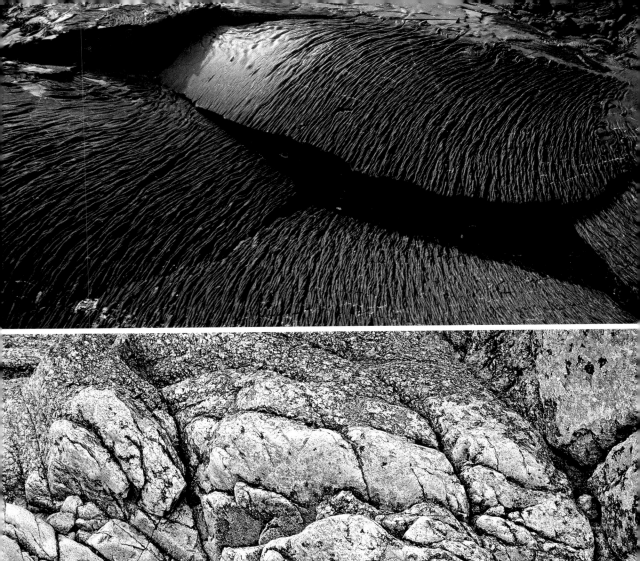

When rocks are broken down and the pieces move somewhere else, it's called erosion (ih-ROH-zhun). These tiny bits of rock and other matter, called sediment, collect and start to pile up. This is how sedimentary rock begins to form.

Piling Up

Sedimentary rocks are made when smaller bits of rock and matter are pressed together over a long time. As more and more matter piles up, the pressure **cements** the matter together. The sedimentary rock shale is clay that has hardened and turned into rock.

15

Changing Again

Metamorphic rocks have been changed by heat and pressure inside Earth. Igneous and sedimentary rocks get pushed under the surface and heated. They're changed to become metamorphic rock when they're heated to between 572 and 1,292°F (300 and 700°C).

17

Some metamorphic rock has lines, or bands, in it from the pressure. The metamorphic rock slate is made of shale that is **squeezed** and changed by heat from inside Earth. Marble is limestone that has been heated for a long time.

limestone

marble

19

Different Paths

Rocks don't always follow the same path in the rock cycle. Rocks on the surface are worn to sediment and can become sedimentary rocks. Igneous and sedimentary rocks can become metamorphic rocks. All rocks can be melted down to magma and made into igneous rock.

The Rock Cycle

igneous rock

COOLING

EROSION AND PRESSURE

COOLING

MELTING

HEAT AND PRESSURE

MELTING

HEAT AND PRESSURE

HEAT AND PRESSURE

EROSION AND PRESSURE

sedimentary rock

HEAT AND PRESSURE

metamorphic rock

21

GLOSSARY

cement: to stick or glue together

crystal: a strong, hard form with atoms in a regular arrangement

igneous: rock made by cooled melted rock

metamorphic: rock changed by heat and pressure

pressure: a force that pushes on something

sedimentary: rock formed when bits of rock and matter are pressed together tightly

squeeze: to press something tightly

FOR MORE INFORMATION

BOOKS

Dee, Willa. *Earth's Rock Cycle*. New York, NY: PowerKids Press, 2014.

Lawrence, Ellen. *What Is the Rock Cycle?* New York, NY: Bearport Publishing, 2015.

Powell, Jillian. *Rock Cycle*. London, UK: Franklin Watts, 2014.

WEBSITES

How Rocks & Minerals Are Formed
rocksforkids.com/RFK/howrocks.html
Discover more facts about rocks and Earth's crust here.

The Rock Cycle
kidsgeo.com/geology-for-kids/0025B-rock-cycle.php
Learn more about how rocks change form on this site.

INDEX